The Question

A survivor's guide for tweens and teens

By Malachi Douglas

Edited by Pamela Francis

The Question
copyright © 2014 Malachi Douglas
and Clay Jars Publishing

This is a work of nonfiction, and no part of the
book or any illustrations may be used, except for
brief excerpts in a review, without written permission from

Clay Jars Publishing
2152 Ralph Avenue #414
Brooklyn, NY 11234
http://www.clayjarspublishing.com

Illustrations copyright © 2013
by John Tinsley and
Clay Jars Publishing
Book designed by Aidana WillowRaven

The author can be reached via email at:
malachismomm@gmail.com

Library of Congress Control Number: 2014939243
ISBN-13: 978-0-9843369-2-0

Printed in the United States of America

LETTER FROM THE EDITOR

Problems in the lives of teens and young people have always been around. "Peer pressure", "bullying" and "adolescence" are buzzwords child psychologists toss around like so many sound bites on "TeenNN" in describing what kids go through in their daily lives, but today's school-aged children may face more than any previous generation in the way of cultivating and maintaining a healthy self-regard. The kind that stands up against questionable media images, a dearth of positive role models, and an increased intimacy with violence, crime and death.

My son's book, "The Question" asks the hard question some parents aren't prepared to answer, and one they probably don't want to hear out of the mouths of the offspring they adore. Bravely willing to disclose his own vulnerability and crisis of faith, Malachi poses a philosophical question to the guardians of his future and finds answers that he can chew over, digest, or even spit out in his quest for personal truth.

The Question

PART I: What's the Use?

    This book started in 2011 when I was in the third grade. I was having trouble with "my peers". I was being messed with. Like one time this kid named Christopher squirted water in my face. Other times kids would do things like flip

The Question

me off when the duty aide wasn't looking.

Stuff like this really messed with me and it just kept happening. I started to have a bad attitude about school, because, after all, I had to go there every day. The fact that the same bullying problem was happening to other kids made me wonder if there was even a reason for being alive. I asked myself, "why do we have to live with so many problems? What's the use of being alive if so many bad things are going to keep happening?"

That's how this book got started. My mom told me to make a list of family and friends I loved and admired. I wrote their names down one by one. Then she gave me her cell phone and told me to call them.

CHAPTER ONE: POP

Pop is my great grandfather. He lives in South Carolina. He works as a preacher and a bus driver. On Saturdays he usually lets me do yard work with him. Some yard work includes mowing the lawn, shaping the bushes, taking the trash to the garbage disposal/recycle center, cutting the weeds, and occasionally raking the leaves. The fun times I have with Pop happen during yard work, or when we go to the store together and when I go to events with him.

Pop is loved so much because he is a sweet, kindhearted, selfless and spiritual person. He is kind to you no matter what, and always loving in his personality. When I asked him The Question, Pop said, "If other students curse or disrespect you, don't fight, just remember to not be afraid to tell the teacher." He also told me to stop wishing I were dead. He said, "Remember to be strong and don't cry, because if you cry, other kids will think it's easy to mess with you, or they will think of you as weak." He reminded me that

The Question

I know the Lord. Pop said, "Remember what we have taught you about the Lord and how He loves you and watches over you."

Pop's advice made me think that I should stay strong and tell the teacher if someone is bothering me instead of fighting or wishing I was dead. I no longer felt hopeless and defeated by my problems at school. I began to let teachers know what was going on with me. I began to feel brave and strong.

A word from the Editor

It's very hard for many adults to hear the actual and often astounding things the young people in their lives are saying. Because Pop drives a school bus I would venture to say that he is in close personal contact with kids of different ages at least twice a day. It is part of his job to write down whenever there are occurrences on the bus that school authorities and parents should be aware of, and I can personally recall how he struggled to articulate in writing some things that had taken place on the bus, whether a physical confrontation between students or the use of bad language directed at himself. I feel that Pop's answer sidestepped the question in favor of providing a solution to something he felt could be concretely dealt with: the bullying. I feel like the philosophical question of how one reconciles themselves with the reality of "bad things happening" in a life was left unhandled, and I wondered if Malachi was at all comforted by the reminder that he "knows the Lord".

From my vantage point as an educator and a mom, the gem in Pop's answer to The Question was his advice not to engage in violence, to enlist the aid of adults, to not give in to negative thought patterns, and lastly, to stay connected with the Source of all: the Creator.

The Question

Survival Guide

- Stand apart -- Don't join the bad behavior you see around you
- Get adults to help you
- Don't give in to negative thoughts and ideas
- Be around people who can give you direction about who God is

CHAPTER TWO: DAD

My dad is a kind, friendly and spiritual person. He is always trying to meet new people and set up Social Business. For example: selling concert tickets, DVDs, CDs and creating careers with different people.

He always takes me to the movies, toy stores and mosques.

My dad is loved and admired because his whole expression is friendly, he's creative, and he always smiles when he meets new people.

My dad said that the only one who can predict that bad things may or may not happen to you is God, so don't believe that bad things will happen to you. "Remember that you're special," he told me, "and you don't need anyone to tell you how you are, who you are, or what you can or cannot do."

When I returned to school I remembered that no one, except for the teacher, can tell me what, how, when or where I can do something, and that you should not believe that bad things will happen to you or not happen to you, and to especially **REMEMBER THAT YOU ARE SPECIAL.**

The Question

A word from the Editor

Malachi's father instilled in him that he was special and that he should keep that information somewhere close to the forefront of his mind. I find this kind of encouragement to be so wanted and needed in the life of young people. In a society where looking, acting, speaking, dancing, dressing and thinking like someone else is demanded of our children in an almost "choose-someone-to-copy-or-die" rush to belong, tweens and teens need to know that who they already are is more than good enough.

The Question

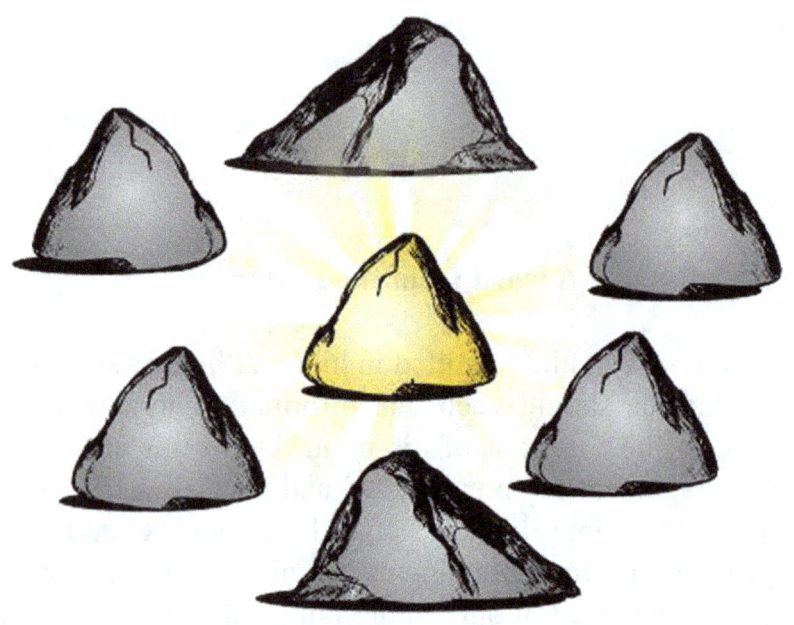

Survival Guide

- Stay close to people who see the value in you
- Cultivate relationships with people who are encouraging of the real you
- Find out what is special about you and protect that

CHAPTER THREE: AUNT PATSI

"Aunt" Patsi is not really my aunt. She is the mother of "Aunt" Coco, one of my mom's friends. She is also a friend of my mom's herself. Aunt Patsi is a kind, sweet, loving person. She likes to make jokes and laugh with my mom. Sometimes my mom does business with her, and sometimes we all just hang out.

Aunt Patsi is motherly and encouraging. She's nice, she's spiritual, and interactive. One time my mom and I went to her house and spent the night. She gave me hot chocolate. She let me dance around as much as I wanted in her house, and watch tv.

Aunt Patsi's answer to the question was, "you make good things happen for yourself." She said, "You don't know that bad things are going to happen. For example, [my daughter] Coco makes good things happen to herself all the time."

After Aunt Patsi's advice, I began to remind

myself that you do not know that bad things will or won't happen to you. I kept in mind that you can make good things happen or not happen for yourself, like "Aunt" Coco.

The Question

Survival Guide

- Become aware of your own God-given power to create the life you want
- Believe in your ability to make good things happen

CHAPTER FOUR: GRANDMA SHIRLEY

Grandma Shirley's personality is very playful. She is funny, cool, loving and very understanding. She always tries to have some sort of fun with me.

Grandma Shirley is a writer. She is loved and admired because of her kind-hearted personality and because she is so encouraging. She helps me with my problems and questions in life. She is truly a great grandmother.

Grandma Shirley said, "bad things will sometimes happen. Sometimes they even make you stronger. God has made us all and given each one of us a purpose," she said. "We all just need to find it. Everything in the universe has a purpose. If you don't know what your purpose is," she added, "Ask God to show you. Ask God why am I here?"

From Grandma Shirley's advice, I learned that bad things happening can even have a good purpose to them, like making you stronger in

The Question

your head and in your heart, or helping someone else to make a better choice. I also learned that everyone or thing in the entire universe has a purpose; we just need to find out what it is.

The Question

Survival Guide

- Try to live a life of purpose
- Be around people who are about their purpose

PART II: How to Deal

By the time I asked Auntie Kahja The Question, two years had gone by since my third grade school issues. I was about to be an eleven year-old fifth grader. I had had my bike stolen, lost my favorite and super expensive Playstation Portable – TWICE -- , been rejected at auditions, been moved across country away from family and friends, and been pulled out of karate class just when I'd become an orange belt. I really knew about "bad" things happening now. The answer to The Question became more important than ever.

CHAPTER FIVE: AUNTIE KAHJA

Auntie Kahja is my mom's sister. She works at an eyeglass shop in Atlanta, Georgia. Sometimes I spend the night at her house and other times we meet at places for dinner and fun times. Auntie Kahja was the one who took me on my first ever trip to the big aquarium in Atlanta.

Auntie Kahja has a playful personality. She is very caring and always hopes the best for me. She always tries to make me feel happy. She has this thing where she can make a song out of anything someone says – in fact, she can come up with the right song that goes with any comment or conversation! She makes everyone laugh when she does this.

When I asked her The Question the first thing she said was that sometimes things are not "bad" even though we might be calling them bad. She said that sometimes things we want to call bad are actually blessings. She gave an example of losing a job ("bad") and then finding a better one (blessing). Then she said that when things happen that really are bad, we can be an example to others in how we handle and react to them. She said that we can be of help to others as they watch the way we go through "bad" things happening. Auntie Kahja said that it was worth living even if bad things happen, because the opportunity to serve or help others using our experiences is always there.

Auntie Kahja's advice changed the way I look at "bad" things. I began to see that some bad things aren't what they seem. I began to look at life as an opportunity to help others and therefore not something to get out of just because things aren't going my way.

The Question

Survival Guide

- Keep at least 1 wise person close in your life
- Let yourself be mentored by a wise person

CHAPTER SIX: AUNT JOHANNA

Aunt Johanna is my mom's friend. She is actually more like a sister to my mom. She was there in the delivery room when my mom gave birth to me. Aunt Johanna likes to have fun and go on adventures. She's a libra, just like me. She is really cool. Me and my mom meet her in different places a lot to hang out, have brunch and other events. My first ever trip to San Francisco was to visit her when she used to live there. Since then she has lived and traveled all over even in Thailand!

Aunt Johanna is loved and admired because she's good-spirited and always is easygoing. She is especially outgoing and nice to people. Her message to me when I asked her The Question was that life is an adventure and that it wouldn't be fun if it weren't for those things we couldn't predict. Things that were awesome, and things that could break your heart. She said that the "bad" things could be looked at as lessons that helped shape the adventure. She said that we have to look at and handle and move the "bad" things as part of our life adventure. She said she wouldn't want to play a game of life if it didn't have adventure.

After talking to Aunt Johanna, I felt like my point of view had been perfected once again into thinking that life is an adventure. It made me realize that the whole "bad thing" life cycle is there for a reason: to KEEP THE ADVENTURE FUN.

The Question

A word from the Editor

I have to say I was truly taken with Johanna's answer. The first thing I appreciated was that she didn't try to convince Malachi that "bad" things don't happen. Rather, she acknowledged that unfortunate and unwanted things do happen to us, and that in order to stay willing and enthusiastic about life in the face of this, we might try looking at life as an adventure with conflicts and obstacles to be navigated and that these increased our enjoyment of the "game" or adventure.

The Question

Survival Guide

- Look at life as an adventure
- Participate in sports and games to get used to winning and "losing" with grace

CHAPTER SEVEN: UNCLE HAKIM

My Uncle Hakim is a musician who lives in New York. Many times when I have called someone Aunt or Uncle in this book, they have not been actual family members, but Uncle Hakim is really my mom's younger brother. Uncle Hakim is fun and gentle and is really the only male in my life who plays with me. I remember going on walks with him and playing games with him at my great grandparents' house.

When I asked him The Question, he told me, "We all know bad things happen but bad things are not the only things that happen. What if good things happened all the time? How do you think that would be?" He said, "you wouldn't even learn anything. You wouldn't even know what a good thing was if it wasn't for the bad."

After talking to my uncle, I learned to keep welcoming the good things, but not be afraid of the bad.

The Question

Survival Guide

- Practice balance in life
- Observe how you feel when "good" things are going on and how you feel when "bad" things are going on, and then do mostly the things that attract "good".

CHAPTER EIGHT: UNCLE RENO

"Uncle" Reno is an actor and a fitness coach. He is a great role model and an even better "uncle".

Uncle Reno is loved and admired because he shows lots of care to people. He lets everyone be themselves and express their own personal style. He's funny, cool and knows how to relate to everyone, especially kids. When I lived in California Uncle Reno always invited me over to fun events at his house.

When I asked him The Question he said, "You don't know that bad things are going to happen. Some "bad" things happen so better things can happen. They're blessings in disguise. Then he told me a story about how the legendary basketball player Michael Jordan had to get through a really rough experience in his sports career that some people would have considered "bad" and how that shaped him into becoming one of the best basketball players of all time. Uncle Reno said that sometimes the feeling that something bad is happening is just fear.

The Question

He asked me, "When something bad happens how do you look at it? If two people walk down the street and see a dead bird, one could go, 'dang, that bird is dead.' And the other could say, 'yeah, that's a spirit that has been set free.' So it's how you look at it; it's perspective. Life is how you look at it."

Uncle Reno's message made me think "bad things" are how you look at them and that some "bad things" can create opportunities and chances for a better life or more joy.

The Question

Survival Guide

- Practice optimism
- Be a person who sees the good in things

CHAPTER NINE: "DAD"

My stepdad is a designer. He works at Home Depot. He is kind of like my male developer. In the past and even now he has been me and my brother's only babysitter. He is very hard-working and cares about me a lot. He can be kind of funny. He is a very unusual dad, but that's why he's great.

His answer to the Question was that we should live even though "bad" things might happen so that we can be part of evolution. He said that humans like the feeling of accomplishment after triumphing over a "bad" thing, and that without "bad" things sometimes happening we wouldn't know we are excellent.

My stepdad's answer was one of the best, if not THE best of all the answers. It's totally true and very brilliant actually. It's all about being a part of evolution, where our species gets better and better at life, and how in the end that leads us to true happiness.

The Question

Survival Guide

- Find something to be excellent at.

Gratitude

I would like to thank the following people who contributed to my book: Shirley Francis-Salley, Rev. Cardell Lindsay, Daymon Douglas, Patsi Simon, Kahja Elliott, Johanna Sweigart, Hakim Francis, Reno Wilson, Guy Oliver West, Kathy Sweigart, Chase Wilmot, Linda Estabrook, Shanea Johnson, Tammy Robbins, Marline Martin, and Dean Washington.

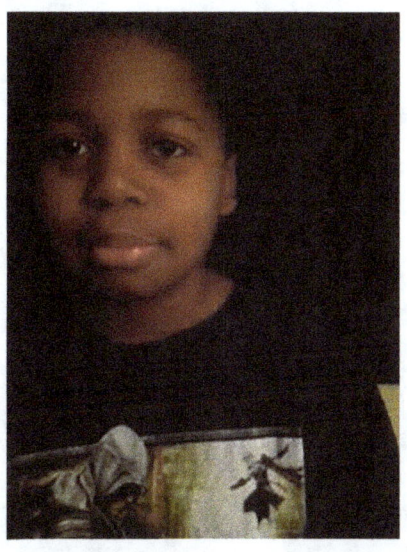

Malachi Douglas is an 11-yr old sixth-grader. He is an artist, an actor, a musician, a jazz enthusiast, a big brother, an orange belt, and an air bender. Malachi lives in Sandy Springs, GA right now, but if you blink... that could change in an instant. And that's just the way he likes it.

John Tinsley is an independent media artist, whose designs have been seen worldwide.

Currently based in Atlanta, Georgia, John works predominantly in graphic design, media marketing, but includes classical illustration in his large-scale installations. His works have been displayed in art shows seen in such locations as The Beehive, Chocolate Chat Atlanta, Centennial Olympic Park, and Saint Joseph's Hospital.

www.ingramcontent.com/pod-product-compliance
Lightning Source LLC
Chambersburg PA
CBHW050609300426
44112CB00013B/2135